# 107 Things I Forgot to Say the Last Time I Talked About:

## Worship, Creativity & Music

BY

# RAY HUGHES

# Thanks

A heartfelt thanks for the generosity and talents of some wonderfully gifted people. Thank you Denise for all the years of sauntering with me. Brian and Ramey Whalen, your endless love and encouragement is priceless. Many thanks to the one and only Sarah Roach for your superb editing and cheerleading skills. And, many many thanks to Amy Fine the world's most amazing personal assistant.

-Ray Hughes

# The Saunterers' Series
## Volume 1

Listening to me as a public speaker has often been described as trying to drink from a fire hose. This journey is a chance for you and I to slow it down. To take our time. To saunter together through thoughts and ideas that I hope inspire revelation and further insight into what has become my life's message.

This is not a textbook on worship, creativity, and music. This is a guided journal that you and I will write together. I have been careful to leave you ample room to journal your insights and revelations regarding each of my entries.
I encourage you to take your time as you walk through the process.

Feel free to start on any page that you like, and go in any direction that appeals to you. Spend as much time as you choose listening to mountains, talking to trees, and singing with birds. I have left you ample room to wander and wonder. Feel free to read a page and not turn to the next page for three months if necessary. If it takes you a week to get from one page to the next, that's ok.

No hurry, no firehose.

This journal is designed to be a journey. It's intended to awaken and restore the lost art of sauntering.

*Saunter* — *(sawn-ter)*
*-- verb*
*1. to walk with a leisurely gait; stroll: sauntering through the woods.*
*-- noun*
*2. a leisurely walk or ramble; stroll.*
*3. a leisurely gait.*
*-- Related forms*
*saun ter er, noun*

Sauntering has become a lost art. It is not necessarily about location — it can be, but it doesn't have to be. It's not about traveling to exotic places in foreign lands and doing adventurous things. It's about turning off the noise in our lives and walking in places where the sound of traffic, television, and commerce fade, and we listen and hear the sound of life. Our life.

This is a compilation of 107 ideas and revelations that can be thought about, pondered, and applied. Some will strike a chord within you that may inspire you to write your own song. You may be inspired to pick up your paintbrush and capture some of the images within the thoughts. Other entries may awaken your inner poet or perhaps cause you to dig deeper as a researcher. Use them as a language for personal worship. Songs and sermons abound in these pages, it will be up to you to mine them out. But, remember, this is not a work-book, this is more about a stroll.

Sometimes to "saunter" means to amble with your hands folded politely behind you, breathing and walking at the peaceful pace of your own heart. Your heart's tempo is a wonderful reminder to fully experience life. This is not a book of lists, scriptures, or formulated ideas and "how to's" about hearing the voice of God. This is an exercise called, "throw your cell phone in your sock drawer and saunter, look, and listen. Slow it all down to see and hear."

While sauntering one day, I wandered into a conversation with a mountain that reminded us both of who we are.

> *I stood as close as I could and looked up, I asked Mountain, what does it feel like to know that nothing stands between you and heaven? He said, "it makes me feel like you."*
>
> *-Ray Hughes*

# 107 Things I Forgot to Say the Last Time I Talked About:

## Worship, Creativity & Music

### BY

# RAY HUGHES

## 1.

If we can change the way that the church understands music and worship, we will change the way the world encounters God.

# Reflections

## 2.

Music is the most majestic form of sound. Sound is the moving of airwaves, and without air we could never hear music. Our first breath brings us into the world as a presence of life. Our last breath takes us out and into eternity. Air is so overlooked, yet it is always secretly near and longing to carry your song.

Let everything that has breath praise the Lord.

# Reflections

# 3.

Every time creativity occurs, God reveals another facet of His nature. His nature is boundless, infinite and indescribably glorious. God desires to reveal Himself to us in ways that no other generation in history has ever seen Him. For us to presume that we already know everything there is to know about Him would be ridiculously arrogant. God delights in using your creative expression to reveal Himself in beautiful and glorious new ways.

# Reflections

# 4.

Gods reveals Himself in and through creation. He created you. How does your creativity reveal Him?

# Reflections

## 5.

God created the earth for you and I to inhabit. So we are inhabiting His creation. He also desires to inhabit our creations in wonderful ways. He desires to be seen and heard and experienced, in our art and songs and handiwork.

# Reflections

# 6.

Sometimes worship songs create an atmosphere that constrains the imagination, protects the politeness of a church service and prevents worship. Sometimes worship songs carry a liberating language that causes people to catch glimpses of God's glory, which increases their yearning to know Him in a deeper way.

# Reflections

7.

Worship-song writers, when you write a worship song, you are not writing next year's popular lyrics. You are creating the next generation's language and understanding of God.

# Reflections

# 8.

God did not become a lawgiver until the worship department started worshiping the works of their own hands. Just sayin'.

# Reflections

# 9.

Sometimes true innovation happens when we simply reinvent what is considered to be unchangeable tradition. Therein lies the difference in innovation and imitation. Dreaming new dreams around old disciplines is a key to innovation. Imitators need to become innovators; otherwise, they are bound to become impostors, doomed to mediocrity.

# Reflections

# 10.

Singers often find themselves emulating the singers who have had the greatest emotional impact upon them. It's perfectly acceptable to do so, and it doesn't have to be kept a secret. Who do you sometimes hear in your head when you sing? Always be grateful for those who have had an influence on you. This will help keep the poison of comparison out of your life.

# Reflections

# 11.

Music, the language of
those that laugh.

Music, the language of
those who live.

Music, the language of
those who long.

Music, the language of
those who love.

# Reflections

# 12.

Live your songs in such a way
that your memories become
melodies and your melodies
become memorable.

# Reflections

# 13.

Renaissance happens when gifted, skilled and knowledgeable thinkers take the time to stop thinking and do the unthinkable.

# Reflections

# 14.

When soul and spirit create
from holy winds of knowings,
love sculpts them into melodies,
and God listens.

When pain and grief hold you
and you look away in silence,
His love does not look away.

God sees.

# Reflections

## 15.

Once upon a moment, God said
yes, the angels laughed, the wind
agreed and a song was born.
You are a song.
Sing your every note.

# Reflections

# 16.

Beyond the narrow parameters of thought, beauty and revelation quietly wait to speak to those who are quiet enough to listen. God made deserts quiet so we could listen and hear.

# Reflections

# 17.

Happiness and sadness are two very real emotions that we all experience from time to time. As Christians we typically insist upon happiness and resist sadness. Yet some of the most beautiful things in our lives are sometimes born out of our darkest and loneliest seasons. There is a delicate veil between beauty and lonesome, so easily torn....

Don't be afraid of times of sadness, for they are some of the best times to sing.

# Reflections

# 18.

Write a song today that you don't want anyone to hear but God.

# Reflections

# 19.

Like creativity, worship is about endless options. It's about the wonder, the beauty, the power, the mercy, the grace, the presence, the infinite, the incomprehensible, the indescribable, the amazing, the magnificent, the glorious person of God.

# Reflections

# 20.

Everywhere there's an expression of worship, there's an opportunity to encounter God. All of creation is worshipping Him right now in ways He cannot resist.

# Reflections

# 21.

Worship can happen when you are singing. Worship can happen listening to your favorite song. Worship can happen in the kitchen. Worship can happen at your desk. Worship can happen in traffic. Worship can happen in your garden. Worship can happen when you are playing with the kids. Worship can happen when you are sewing. Worship can happen on horseback. Worship can happen at the mall. Worship can happen in an airplane. Worship can happen while you are walking. Worship can happen in church. Worship can happen when you let it happen. Worship can happen.

# Reflections

The first person in the Bible who was recorded as being filled with the Holy Spirit wasn't filled so he could give a verbal message, a prophecy or teaching, but so he could create works of art (Bazelel, Exodus 35:30).

# Reflections

# 23.

Live a musical day today.
Choose to create an atmosphere
of awakening in your heart.
Unbridle your imagination and
let your personality and public
politeness yield to passion. Let
the language of your heart and
lyrics of your life be a liberating
musical force everywhere you
go. Fully expect worship to
occur in fresh and wondrous
ways today. Today is a day of
worship. Watch for
opportunities to get loud if
necessary.

# Reflections

# 24.

King David surrounded himself with poets, songwriters, storytellers, musicians, and writers.

# Reflections

# 25.

Worship is an awakening of the heart that carries passionate responses to God's presence.

# Reflections

# 26.

Our generation is being invited to expand our understanding of worship. We are also being invited to express our worship to God in new and glorious ways. When we say yes to His invitation, we can Renaissance-type awakenings and revolutionary ideas full of revelation and life. We need culture-shifting revolutionary worship leaders to step forward.

# Reflections

# 27.

Don't spend this wonderful day longing for God's presence. Expect God's presence, pray God's presence, sing God's presence, dance, play, sculpt, paint God's presence. Your expressed worship is a part of the soundtrack of all creation-- the creation that is worshipping Him right now in ways He cannot resist.

# Reflections

# 28.

Worship in spite of your weariness.
Praise louder than your pain.
Our circumstances do not make God
any less worthy or wonderful.

# Reflections

# 29.

If you are devoid of passion for
the life that you live, look into
your heart until you find a
memory or a dream. Not just
any memory or any dream--

Find one so beautiful that it
makes you whisper.
When you can no longer
whisper, go ahead and sing.

Your heart will do the rest.

# Reflections

# 30.

When you begin to live your life
from a place of passion,
You awaken possibilities and
options that never see you
coming until they are caught in
the midst of your whirlwind,
Not knowing should they sing
or dance.

# Reflections

## 31

Psalm 50:2 states, "Out of Zion, the perfection of beauty, God has shone forth."
All of the beauty and wonder that we see and experience in this fallen world is imperfect and merely a dim reflection of the "perfection and beauty of God."

# Reflections

## 32.

Every time you go to church, ask yourself this question:

"Why am I going?"

Obligation to church or fascination with God? The answer won't just change the way you do church--

It will change the way you do life.

# Reflections

# 33.

Forceful exhalation through partially closed vocal cords and lips produces what pulmonary doctors call "P.E.E.P" (Post End Expiratory Pressure). Lung patients are encouraged to do this exercise because it increases oxygenation of the blood as it circulates around the alveoli. This simple procedure holds open the alveoli sacs in your lungs that otherwise collapse. Another name for this process is "singing." Singing for twenty minutes a day boosts your immune system and increases your life expectancy. So walking and singing twenty minutes a day will change your life. It will not only change the way you live, but also change how long you get to do it. Lord you are the strength of my life, and you are my song.

# Reflections

# 34.

You think you're not creative? You are. You may not be artistic, but you are creative. Everything that God ever created is creative. Wind creates more wind, water creates more water, trees create more trees, grass creates more grass, flowers create more flowers, fire creates more fire. Fifty thousand cells in your body will die and recreate new cells in the time that it takes you to read this sentence. The Creator created you to be creative. I wonder how many other expressions of your God-given creativity you might be overlooking?

# Reflections

# 35.

There is a certain amount of personal fulfillment and elation that comes with achieving some amount of skill and artistry. However, if you are only using your artistic expression for overcoming a sense of personal insignificance and finding self-importance, you are not experiencing God's best for your art or your life. Both are pitiful reasons for expressing your art, and both can trap you in a deep mire of self-centeredness.

# Reflections

# 36.

God designed music, worship, and creativity to awaken the true you to experience the true Him. Abandon the boundaries you have erected around your personality. Today is the day that you cease to protect yourself by guarding your dreams and hiding your heart. Today is the day to sing the new song that *is* the new you. Creativity, music, and true worship happen when silence tells its dreams. For art, especially music, is the most confident voice of silence. Tell God your dreams as a part of your expressed discipline. Sing your dreams, paint your dreams, dance your dreams, write your dreams, sculpt or carve or make jewelry while you dream out loud. Turn your pottery wheel into a dream machine. Dream in every key or chord or note that you can play on your instrument. Let the true you break the silence today. Let God hear the true you--out loud--as a vocabulary of worship.

# Reflections

## 37

Truth and beauty are always
dressed in simplicity and
wonder.
What you believe to be
beautiful in your life will always
find its way into your art.

If you will let it be simple, God
will make it wonderful.

# Reflections

# 38.

Samuel to Saul:

"When the musicians play, you
will be changed."

# Reflections

## 39.

Music is a time and place for God's presence. Go to a symphony and sit and silently worship God. Go to a secular concert and praise God and pray for those who are performing. Celebrate and thank God for the gift of music you see in their lives. If you have an opportunity to meet them, the best thing you can do for them is honor them with authentic kindness. No flattery allowed.

# Reflections

## 40

A song can go away and out of your life. Then, one day, it suddenly rushes in unexpectedly and brings a thousand memories home. A good song always remembers you, knows where you are, and somehow knows when you need to remember.

# Reflections

# 41.

Worship is about expressing the passion of your heart. Do it purposefully and consistently, with authentic and honest intent of heart.

It's not just a lifestyle--it's life.

# Reflections

# 42.

Ask the Lord for supernatural grace to be a praise in the earth in your generation.

What does that mean to you at this time in your life?

# Reflections

# 43.

Music resonates and illuminates the mind.  It lights shadowy places so the thoughts and meditations of your heart are welcomed to come out of hiding.

# Reflections

## 44.

Psalmists carry stories of the victories and faithfulness of God throughout the generations. Their language accesses the presence and power of God through lyrical expressions of praise. Be a psalmist.

# Reflections

# 45.

Listening to music is an important part of the journey of life.

There is something missing in your life if most of the music you hear is recorded.

# Reflections

## 46.

In the midst of nothingness, God revealed the vastness of His creative nature.

Evidently an empty canvas in an empty, silent space is a good place to do wondrous things.

# Reflections

# 47.

We are created in God's image, and He is a wonder and a mystery. He defies intellectual reasoning, and so should we. Our creativity should challenge and stimulate the intellect, but we shouldn't be bound or limited by our intellect. Unleash your intuition and imagination. Look at all the outlandish and imaginative things God has created. Ask Him who is able to do exceedingly abundantly above all that we ask or think according to the power that works in us to direct your imagination.

# Reflections

# 48.

Whether your particular discipline is opera, ballet, woodcarving, or knitting, artistic disciplines should be challenging, rewarding, and saturated in honest humility. And, just for fun, leave the knowing to the One who knows all things. Go ahead and defy intellectual reasoning and awaken your outrageous imagination and worship Him according to your passionate, creative heart. Then go tell someone about it.

# Reflections

# 49.

Challenge yourself. Potters do poetry, poets do pottery, singers dance, dancers sing, sculptors write a song, tambourine players take a day off. (Haha)

# Reflections

## 50.

It's perfectly acceptable to challenge man's boundaries and limitations that strive to define "acceptable" art. Your creative expression is meant to defy systematic reasoning, cultural acceptance and religious restrictions. That's what worship does.

# Reflections

# 51.

It's okay to explore the colors and notes without fully knowing what the outcome will be. After all, colors and notes are where it all began.

# Reflections

## 52.

True creativity is born out of God's desire to reveal His mysteries. He reveals Himself in and through creation. His nature is wondrous and mysterious. He not only reveals Himself through His creative process, but also reveals Himself through *our* creative process.

# Reflections

# 53.

Our creativity can never find its full expression in the confines of man's intellect. It's wonderful to know about God and yet more wonderful to know God. To sense that you are experiencing spontaneous moments and thoughts with a timeless, all-knowing, all-encompassing, eternal God is an awesome reality that defies intellectual reasoning. It is more than knowing about Him. To imagine that our Creator wants us to partner with Him in creativity speaks of who He is more than we can know.

# Reflections

## 54.

The more we learn about God's creation, the more opportunities we find to marvel at Him. What a marvelous God!

# Reflections

# 55.

Self-promotion...self-denial
Self-centeredness...self-sacrifice
Self-importance...self-esteem
Self-indulgence...self-discipline
Self-destruction...self-control
Self-conscious...self-worth

Watch your *self*; life can be tedious.

# Reflections

# 56.

We have greatest access to Him and His wonderful mysteries in atmospheres of worship.

# Reflections

# 57.

Consider the brush in your hand
or the guitar on your lap to be a
tool that can help enable you
and others to embrace God and
all His mysterious possibilities.

# Reflections

# 58.

Remember that worship and worship services are not always the same thing.

# Reflections

# 59.

Treat your dreams like promises.
If one is broken, forgive
yourself.

# Reflections

# 60.

Do you feel that you have become a wounded soul and you are unable to fully live your life as a creative, inspired, and inspiring person? Or maybe you require a cascade of daily affirmations and validation just to survive.

Sometimes life just requires a very simple recalibration. So today, love God, trust God, and do your very best to give Him your whole heart as a worshipper. Put first things first and other things nowhere.

# Reflections

# 61.

In the beginning God chose a
canvas of darkness to paint light
and life, and His words became
matter and mystery.

# Reflections

# 62.

Start with what you have--*nothing* is a good place to begin.

# Reflections

# 63.

Upon a canvas of darkness, light and life were painted as matter and mystery. Words became hope and were carried to man in the form of dreams, filled with possibilities. Find new ways to express words of hope today. Bring light to dark places in your life and the lives of others.

# Reflections

# 64.

Praise and worship are the
intent of heart, expressed.
Worship can be a lyric or a
note, a stroke of a brush or
piece of chalk or pen.

# Reflections

# 65.

Music activates, stimulates, and uses the entire brain. It can bypass the intellect and have a profound impact on your spirit. It can also affect your physical body, as every cell in your body responds to music. Saturate your whole being today-- Spirit, soul, and body.

# Reflections

# 66.

Whenever you feel like you fit
in a lyric more than you fit in
life...Sing.
Life is not always about feeling
like you fit...Sing.

How do you feel now?  It
doesn't matter...Sing.

# Reflections

# 67.

Music is emotion in motion, and sometimes the fewer the notes played, the more beauty you hear. Nothing captures the heart like the wonder and power of well-played silence. Lord help us to value the beauty of silence when we worship.

# Reflections

# 68.

Music is a vital to the human experience. Music is universal, song is geographical, and melody is topographical. Cultures and subcultures are defined and identified with the term *sound*: "Nashville Sound," "Delta Blues" as opposed to "Chicago Blues," "Muscle Shoals Sound," "Mountain Sound," "Tibetan Sound." Where you live, and how you live, should also be about why you live, musically speaking. How do you respond creatively to your landscape, your city and your culture? Is your love for God's presence enriched by your love of a place? Do you live in a place that awakens your creativity and calls you to worship? Music knows where you live. It also knows where you came from.

# Reflections

# 69.

Music doesn't just touch your senses, stimulate thought and awaken memories. Dance doesn't just engage your physical body in movement and self-expression. Art doesn't just bring color and texture and image to canvas. Writing and storytelling are not just literary and verbal communication mechanisms designed to convey thought and emotions and dispense information. These are not just forms of creativity and personal expression either. These are gifts that help our human-ness and our true heaven-ness find one another. They awaken us to life and cause our heart, imagination, wonder, beauty, mystery, sadness, pain and joy to find one another and dance the most elegant steps of life.

# Reflections

# 70.

Music is a call for your spirit to awaken your soul to an eternal dance. It's an ancient dance, too beautiful for your body to know. Its steps are too broad and its leaps are too explosive to be contained in well-managed lives, linear identities, and physical boundaries. This dance of the heart ushers you past religious rules and Christian rhetoric. A dance of the heart cannot be limited by lifeless liturgy and lofty language. It introduces you to a new understanding of His holiness as you encounter the wonderful wildness of God.

# Reflections

# 71.

Worship is not about having an informed mind. It's about having an inflamed heart.

# Reflections

# 72.

Could it be that times of upheaval in our lives are just our smothered souls and longing spirits attempting to break out of confusion and thoughts of forsakenness to try to be all that we long to be?

# Reflections

# 73.

Music reminds our spirit and soul of who they really are, for music arises out of the simultaneous desires of heaven and earth.

# Reflections

## 74.

To understand your value as a "creative" is to have a sense that you are created to do something that no one else has done, because no one else can.

# Reflections

# 75.

Sights, sounds and symbols create significance and identity. As Americans, we pay tribute to significance and acknowledge identity every time we sing our National Anthem. Every nation has a national anthem, a national dance, a national bird, a national flower. All of these sounds and images were created to help us celebrate our sense of national identity. We are known and recognized all over the earth by the sights, sounds and symbols that mark us as Americans. Consider the skill and creativity that has gone into the American flag, the Liberty Bell, the Statue of Liberty. Look at the images depicted in the lyrics of our National Anthem. O say, can you see what's being said? It is universally true. What we consistently celebrate creatively marks us and gives us our identity. Creativity is a celebration. What, when, where, and who do you celebrate? In what, when, where, and in who do you find your identity?

# Reflections

# 76.

You will have approximately 70,000 thoughts today. If life brings something to your attention, at least ask it if it's a song, a painting, a poem or a prophecy. Accessing possibilities is a part of the creative process. It requires an acknowledging and an awakening to those possibilities. Simply put, pay attention to your thoughts. Some are meant to be stewarded, shaped and fashioned into art.

# *Reflections*

## 77

Music is an enchanting force that reminds us of forgotten moments that somehow lost their significance along the way. Beautiful music can reawaken memories to an even greater significance in your life. Sing a melody that causes you to remember something wonderful that God has done in your life.

# Reflections

# 78.

My guitar is a friend...When we talk, music happens.

My paintbrush is a friend...When we talk, art happens.

My pen is a friend...When we talk, poetry happens.

My voice is a friend...When I sing, prayer happens.

# Reflections

## 79.

If you have a mission without a message, you will always default to performance.

# Reflections

# 80.

Much of creative culture, including Christian culture, is built on labels and mistaken identities. We formulate unrealistic responsibilities and expectations and impose them upon our personal gifting. That's where mistaken identities come from. Choose this day to be who you really are. You are foremost a worshipper.

# Reflections

# 81.

Today is a really good day to be.
So, Just be.

# Reflections

# 82.

God is eternal…

When you pray, see the future.

When you sing, create the
future.

When you worship, invade the
future.

# Reflections

## 83

Psalm 33:3 *Sing* unto the Lord a *new* song.

שִׁיר *shiyr*

Verb, *sheer.*

A primitive root for this word *sing* comes to us from the idea of strolling minstrelsy. It was also used in the context of street harlots and merchants letting their intentions be known in the streets and marketplace. It means to sing and also to behold. Your song is not about prostituting yourself or merchandising. Your song is about walking out the intentions of your life as a song unto the Lord.

# Reflections

# 84.

A "new" song.

חָדַשׁ *chadash*

Verb, *khaw-dash.*

This comes from a primitive root
word that means to be new; to
rebuild--renew, repair and restore
and make new. You as well as
those in your path could probably
use some renewing, restoring,
rebuilding and refreshing lyrics,
sounds and rhythms, new songs
void of any intentions of
prostitution and merchandising.
It's perfectly acceptable, and even
necessary, to be heard and seen
(beheld) as you take your music to
the marketplace. Just be careful
that your intent is *UNTO THE
LORD.*

# Reflections

# 85.

Kingdom-minded "creatives" no longer have permission to bury their gifts in lands of empty churches and full theaters. The church has consistently lived twenty years behind the cutting edge of creativity long enough.

# Reflections

# 86.

Right now heaven is resonating with boundless grace and unlimited creativity. Our generation is being gloriously invaded with songs and sounds. The overflow of heaven is becoming the melodies and rhythm and lyrics of a generation.

# Reflections

# 87.

Beautiful music always resembles a new beginning. It is part quickening, part awakening. It is silence being lovingly broken.

# Reflections

## 88.

Dark, angry music is not really music. It's wind that has lost its way and insists upon pulling hearts into its storm. Passion and anger are two very different sounds.

# Reflections

# 89.

Music demands multi-generational responses. What is your response to your grandparents' music, parents' music, children's music? As a father, something special happens in your life when you realize that you are amazed by the things that amazed your father. Spend some time exploring the music that captured the love and attention of those who came before you.

# Reflections

# 90.

The song that we leave for the next generation is what enables us to sing of His mercies forever. What one generation sows in faith, the next generation can reap in favor. So sing your songs as if every song was your last opportunity to sow the seeds of your life into the earth.

Psalm 89:1

# Reflections

# 91.

Worship leaders, the greatest tool you have for leading others in worship is the overflow of your personal worship.

# Reflections

# 92.

When God is speaking, we have an opportunity to respond or to react to His voice. To respond is to step closer; to react is to step away. To respond creatively is to embrace.

# Reflections

## 93

One of the worst things that can happen to someone destined for greatness is to become held prisoner by fame. Greatness never comes to those who look for it, but greatness will seek and find those whose dream is to give.

# Reflections

# 94.

Sometimes songwriters live too much of their lives somewhere between memory and imagination, looking for opportunities to sing what they have seen.

# Reflections

# 95.

A dewdrop does the will of God just as much as a thunderstorm. It's okay to be a note—you don't have to be a symphony.

# Reflections

## 96.

God created us to be image-bearing worshippers who carry the sound from nation to nation and land to land, tribe to tribe and tongue to tongue. Don't overlook the kitchen and living room.

# Reflections

## 97

Singing is nothing more than impassioned speech. When you encounter something that makes you so passionate that you just have to sing, you have found some of the notes that make up your song.

# Reflections

# 98.

Real music *occurs*. It usually happens when your noisy mind yields to the quiet beauty that lives in your heart.

# Reflections

# 99.

We are a people designed and created to worship. If we don't worship our God, we forfeit the reason we exist.

# Reflections

# 100.

We are all a part of a musical production because we are a part of the universe.

Uni= one, and verse= song.

One song. Sing your note today.

# Reflections

# 101.

Sing new songs to the Lord only on the days that His mercies are new.

# Reflections

# 102.

Old cycles are being broken
because new songs are being
sung.
New songs break old cycles.

# Reflections

# 103.

God loves to storm atmospheres of worship and prayer with a sound of a rushing mighty wind. If God's voice can shake earth, can our voices shake heaven?

When we sing our worship to God, I wonder if heaven hears the sound of a rushing mighty wind. Either way, it's time for the house of God to shake again.

I wonder if heaven is waiting for a shaking too. Let's storm the atmosphere of heaven and see.

# Reflections

# 104.

The difference between a nightmare and a dream is that one lives in the noise of a troubled mind, and one lives in the song of an awakened heart.

# Reflections

105.

Fan-based Christianity has very little effect on an ego-driven culture because it rarely demonstrates God's heart for hurting humanity--too many lights and not enough love.

# Reflections

## 106

David was a shepherd, a musician, a singer, a songwriter, a giant slayer, a warrior, a prophet, a king, a father, a son, a sinner, a repenter, and a passionate worshipper.

# Reflections

# 107.

The two most important prerequisites for worship leaders…

1.  A fire in your heart that will not go out to worship God.

2.  A fire in your heart that will not go out to see others worship God.

# Reflections

For More
Information
Contact Us At:

Selah Ministries

P.O. Box 16917
Asheville, NC 28816

www.selahministries.com

selah.ministries@yahoo.com